The Funeral Book

by
Clarence W. Miller

Robert D. Reed, Publishers • San Francisco, California

Robert D. Reed, Publishers
750 La Playa, Suite 647 • San Francisco, California 94121
Telephone: 1-800-PR-GREEN

Editing by Pamela D. Jacobs, M.A.
Book Design & Typesetting by Kaye Graphics
Cover by Joseph E. Haga
Cover Art by Timothy J. Strickling

Printed by Gilliland Printing
Distributed by Login Publishers Consortium
Telephone: (312) 733-8228 / Fax: (312) 733-3107

Library of Congress Cataloging-in-Publication Data

Miller, Clarence W.
      The funeral book / by Clarence W. Miller.
            p.   cm.
      ISBN 1-885003-02-1 : $7.95
      1. Funeral rites and ceremonies—United States—
      Handbooks, manuals, etc.   I. Title.

      GT3203.M45   1994
      393—dc20   94-18801
                                                                                CIP

Designed, Typeset, and Manufactured
in The United States of America.

Dedication

To my mother, **Violet**, who taught me to always live by The Golden Rule.

And to my two daugthers, **Kelly** and **Kandy**, who encouraged me to write this book.

Contents

Chapter 1

Funerals, Who Needs Them?

"To everything there is a season and a time to every purpose under the heaven. A time to be born, and a time to die."

Ecclesiastes Chapter 3, verses 1 & 2

Funerals aren't for everyone, but the ceremony has a purpose and is beneficial for most people. I have often heard and, I'm sure you have also, the phrase "Funerals are barbaric!"

Actually, it's just the opposite. It is barbaric not to honor the dead. Barbarians just left the dead where they lay, in most cases. They cared little about their dead.

It's a fact that the "most" civilized early men always had some type of burial rites.

The American people, with diverse cultures from all over the world, have many different needs to be met through various funeral rites.

In this book I will, through my eyes, explain a few of these rites and provide some inside information on funeral services, ways to save money and behind-the-scenes practices that have been hidden from the public. I will explain it in simple language that is easy to understand.

No one likes funerals, but a formal ending to a life worth remembering is important so "other lives" can continue. The living must go on.

Funeral rites vary the world over. Customs in the jungles of Africa or South America are very different from those in New York, Los Angeles, Chicago, London or Moscow. One thing all have in common: when a death occurs, three important basic tasks need to be done.

First, the body must be washed, refrigerated, wrapped, placed in a body bag, embalmed or handled in some other manner.

Second, a decision must be made on what to do with the body. Some people prefer to pray over it and some just remember the life that had been lived. Others try to get someone else to make all the difficult decisions and to handle arrangements for them.

And third, last and most difficult, the body must be deposed. Someone must take it somewhere. It must be put in its final resting place. That place can be a cemetery, the ocean, the wilderness, or even in an urn on the fireplace mantle or in a closet.

In my 35-plus years in the business, I can say no two funeral services are exactly alike. Each person has some idea of what is important to his or her needs. We have the freedom in this country to make our own decisions.

In the past, and still today in some countries, everyone had to conform with the ruling class or the majority of opinion. The founding fathers of the United States provided in our constitution individual choice of lifestyle. With such freedom, our funeral customs have developed over the years and are still developing.

The disposition most people think of is what funeral directors call "traditional." When a death occurs, the family or hospital calls the funeral director. He goes to the place of death, makes removal to the funeral home and embalms the body. Next, the family contacts the funeral home to arrange for a funeral service. This usually means a time of viewing or "wake" for one or two days at the funeral home, a chapel service conducted by a member of the clergy, there or at a church, and concluding graveside services in a local cemetery. There can be many variations from this "traditional" service.

A member of the clergy who is known to the deceased or family is most likely to be called upon to conduct the service, but this isn't necessary. Anyone can officiate. It could be a family member, a family friend, a lodge, the American Legion or Veterans of Foreign Wars Post, or even the funeral director, if so wished. There are no rules on whom to choose.

Today "Graveside Services Only" is a popular option for families. Everything is the same, except services are conducted only at the graveside. This service usually lasts for 10 to 20 minutes.

On occasions when weather prohibits, or if burial is to be at a distant cemetery requiring lengthy transportation, concluding services take place at the funeral home.

If the body is to be shipped a great distance, air transport is most often used. The airlines require the casket to be protected by an airtray—a wooden tray with a cardboard cover around the casket to protect it from damage. Unless you know what to look for, one would only think of it as normal air freight. Anyone who has ever traveled on a commercial airline has no doubt traveled with human remains aboard.

If the cemetery is not too distant (within 1500 miles) the funeral director may handle transport. It is usually less expensive to have the local funeral director handle all services and transport to final disposition. There are firms who contract with funeral homes to provide this type of service exclusively.

When distant air shipment is made a funeral director is required in the receiving city to accept and transport the casket from the airport to the funeral home or cemetery for final services. Chapel services can be arranged, if so wished by survivors, before final graveside services for family and friends there. The original funeral director will make all the arrangements.

Not everyone wants a funeral. If this is one's choice, for whatever reasons, that option should be available.

One can request a "Direct Burial." When there are no services of any kind, the funeral director takes the body to the cemetery as soon as time allows after the necessary paper work is completed and filed with local officials. No new notices are needed, if one chooses. No one needs to know when the burial takes place. Notification is made afterwards in some cases. This is often the case after cremations.

A funeral, of whatever type, is important. Many people do not see the value of them. Many, even some clergy, talk against the practice until the time comes for one of their loved ones to be put to rest. There is no other way to express a loss, although the custom can vary.

Chapter 2

Embalming, Cosmetics And Dressing

Embalming—what is it? Is it required by law? Why are some deceased embalmed and others are not? What happens in the embalming procedure? These are a few questions that you may ask and want answered.

The number one reason for our customs in taking care of the deceased in this country is health considerations. When a person dies, there are definite needs to be taken care of in a manner that will protect the public health.

On the whole, across the United States, the laws concerning treatment of human remains are similar from state to state. These include handling of contagious diseases, shipment across state lines and refrigeration when the remains are not embalmed.

Embalming is not required by law in most instances. Of course, there are exceptions to every rule. In cases of communicable diseases, for instance, the coroner or medical examiner can order embalming if time is needed to locate survivors. Airlines can require it before shipment to a distant city. All international shipments must be embalmed before proper permits can be obtained. These are just some examples.

In some states, embalming must take place if an open casket service is planned with the public invited. This makes sense. Would anyone want to approach the casket containing the remains of a loved one or friend only to observe them in a deteriorated, unrecognizable condition or detect a very unpleasant odor, closed casket or not? In embalming, the first concern is for disease prevention or sanitation. The second is to delay tissue breakdown when a public funeral will be held at a later time.

The embalming procedure is simple most of the time but sometimes can be very difficult to accomplish. There are many variables to embalming a body, so no two cases are exactly alike. Several things must be done before embalming can begin. Bathing is first and just what it signifies. The body is bathed with soap and water and unwanted hair is shaved whether the body is male or female.

Then, the mouth must be closed. With almost everyone who dies, because of muscle relaxation, the mouth must be closed in a fixed position. This is usually done by wiring the mouth closed, similar to someone with a broken jaw.

An important point to remember is to give, or leave, the deceased's dentures for the funeral director to take at the time of removal. The dentures are of no use whatsoever if one brings them in after embalming has taken place. It is impossible to put dentures in place at that point, and they will be discarded. Most people assume that the dentures can still be placed. This is a common misconception. The funeral director will usually accept the dentures and not say anything for fear of upsetting the family.

The eyelids also must be closed. This is done by inserting "eye caps" under the eyelids. These are plastic, constructed in the shape of the eyes, with raised areas to hold the eyelids in place.

The head is positioned at a slight right angle so that it can be seen more clearly in the casket. The hands usually are placed together at the waist or positioned so that a ring will be visible when on view.

Then the embalming fluid is injected, usually with an incision approximately 2 inches long in an area where major blood vessels are relatively close to the skin's surface. The two most common points are the cartoid (neck) and femoral (upper leg) artery regions.

Some morticians prefer one area to another. This does not make sense to me. I can relate, for a fact, that some funeral home owners insist their embalmers embalm from a particular area of the body. I believe funeral home owners or managers who adhere to this policy are not only on an ego trip, but do not know what they are talking about most of the time. I may get flack from many of them, but that does not change the fact that only the embalmer preparing the case can determine what is best.

After the incision is made, the tissues are separated to expose the jugular vein and cartoid artery. A small incision is made in each to allow introduction of embalming fluid into the artery and drainage of blood from the vein. In other words, the embalming fluid pushes the blood out of the body via the veins.

Think of it as flushing the cooling system of your car. It's the same principle. Embalming is flushing the body and, in the process, the embalming fluids sanitize the body and preserve the cells against premature breakdown until funeral services can be held and burial taken place.

If all things are normal, this procedure is completed in approximately an hour and a half with no problems. A common major problem would be lack of drainage, which results in the body appearing discolored from blood still present in the tissues. There are ways to help overcome this problem, though not always successful.

First, I assess the situation and prepare to raise vessels in alternate areas. Most embalming is done from the right side of the body. That is because it is the side viewed in the casket. So, it is important for the embalmer to look at the body as it will be viewed in the casket.

If drainage is not successful from that side, the embalmer needs to move to the left side and repeat the procedures, hoping drainage will be better there. If that is not successful, I go to the femoral regions on each leg and repeat the procedures.

In most cases, that will clear the head, trunk and legs, but still leaves the arms and hands. It is important to clear these, because they are visible during the wake and funeral service. Under the upper arms, vessels are raised and embalming fluid injected down the arms in an attempt to clear the fingertips. If that fails, an incision can be made on the wrist (where the pulse is taken) and embalming fluid can be injected into the hand until it clears up.

Lack of drainage occurs if there is severe artery disease that prevents good circulation or if too much time elapses between death and embalming. Also, certain medications have an adverse effect on embalming chemicals.

It is sometimes necessary to stop the injection of fluid to prevent swelling—caused by blood clots lodged in small vessels, preventing circulation. Usually, the clots can be dislodged by massage.

There are times when it seems that no matter what is done to embalm a body, nothing goes right. The embalmer can be doing everything right, but nothing works properly. Circulation may be bad and what little there is may be ineffective. When problems of this kind arise, the embalmer usually completes the embalming process with a hypodermic syringe for injection. The best an embalmer can hope for then is preservation.

These problems explain why the funeral director will attempt to get permission to embalm as soon as possible. In most states, the funeral director must get written or oral permission from the next of kin before embalming is permitted. Permission must be documented in the arrangement file.

During the embalming process, there is time to clean fingernails and wash the hair. After embalming is completed, face cream is applied to prevent dehydration until cosmetics are applied at a later time.

There is a wide variety of opinions in the industry on the proper application of cosmetics. Some feel that all the exposed facial surfaces must be completely cosmetized, covering any and all blemishes, moles and scars that may appear on the face.

Most often, makeup is applied so thickly that the deceased is barely recognizable. Morticians who work this way think that their work is beautiful. I believe that this is one reason so many people are opposed to viewing the remains. I agree with them.

The deceased should be left as natural as possible. If a mole appeared on his or her face before death, then it should be present after death. The body should appear to be sleeping. It should not look like a mannequin in a department store window. But no matter what you say to them, some morticians will "cake" on the cosmetics. By their actions, the rest of the industry suffers. If you notice this problem, object to the funeral director. Tell him to remove the excess makeup and leave a natural appearance.

In providing clothing for a loved one, try to remember how that person would want to be dressed. Any type of clothing is acceptable. If the deceased rarely wore a tie or silk blouse, why let some funeral director talk you into buying burial clothing that includes such items? Burial clothing available at most funeral homes is of the lowest quality and of the highest price.

Why not use the deceased's personal clothing? If that person wore jeans and a shirt, why not dress them in like manner? Remember, any and all clothing is acceptable.

If your loved one was always seen wearing an apron, like my mother, then an apron should be part of the burial clothing selection. The same goes for a man. If he was known for wearing bib overalls, then maybe that's what he should be buried in.

I am often asked the question, "Is the clothing cut to make it fit?" Yes, most often it is. Cutting the clothing can make it fit better. There are those who will not cut clothing at any time, but it does fit better when cut. It's a matter of personal choice by the dresser.

Providing a picture of the person in life helps the funeral director to know how the hair should be fixed or parted. Most funeral homes have a beautician on staff to assist them.

Should jewelry be included? Yes, but it should be removed and returned to the family before burial. Why bury something of value when it could be handed down to future generations or other family members? This includes glasses, hearing aids, watches, tie tacs, lodge pins, buttons, etc. Maybe such items do not have monetary value, but I know for a fact that they have sentimental value to survivors. You may choose to donate items such as glasses and hearing aids to civic groups to benefit others who cannot afford them.

If there are certain items that you want to include in the casket with the deceased, then do so. It is acceptable to put anything you wish that will fit into the casket—pictures, letters, notes, favorite flowers, a favorite book, or anything you choose. Always make sure, though, that the other family members don't mind.

Chapter 3

A Casket Or A Coffin?

I am amazed at how little people know about caskets when they come in to make funeral arrangements. Buying a casket is the same as buying any merchandise. There are great differences in quality, style, workmanship and colors.

Usually people pick a casket only by appearance. True, what it looks like is important, but one should consider quality. Often a lesser priced casket is of more value than the one that is higher priced.

"Casket" originally meant "Jewel Box." Look it up in your dictionary. The term "Jewel Box" means it contains something precious. And, I'm sure that one would agree that when a loved one is placed in a casket, that casket does contain something precious. There is nothing more precious in the world than a loved one who is close to your heart.

Caskets are often mistakenly referred to as coffins. You cannot buy a coffin in the United States. They are not manufactured here except by private individuals. Coffins are made in other parts of the world. Technically, both do the same thing, but they are as different as a Volkswagen and a Rolls Royce. A coffin is a different shape. It has six sides, wide at the shoulders and narrow at the feet. This is the original coffin known as a burial container by the layman.

Modern-day coffins are almost always made of wood and imported into the United States. Some may be lined with glass panels for viewing without the body being exposed because of poor embalming procedures or none at all. Others may be lined with lead or tin interiors. But the shape remains the same. Coffins are always six-sided, and caskets are always have a rectangular shape.

Caskets made of plywood, pressed wood, soft wood or pine are most often covered with cloth material. They are available in a range of colors. Quality varies from very simple to most elaborate. Because of their low cost, funeral directors tend to keep few of this type of casket in display rooms. Like a car dealer who wants to sell the most expensive car, the funeral director, for the most part, wants to do the same.

I have managed funeral homes for large corporations that own mortuaries, cemeteries, floral shops, casket companies, finance companies, etc., across the United States and Canada. In every case the head office constantly sent reports on ways to increase the dollar value of caskets, vaults, and flowers sold. The administrators were more interested in making a large profit than in taking care of the needs of the families they were serving.

Let me say here that, for the most part, the employees usually do not agree with the owner's or manager's attitude. In most cases, the manager or owner will pressure the employee to sell the more expensive caskets and other funeral related merchandise, even to the point of giving commissions to motivate larger sales.

During my career, there have been a few owners who have not brought this type of pressure upon employees. There are many sincere directors of locally and family owned funeral homes more interested in serving their community honestly than in how much money they can make. I would suggest to those who may need funeral services in the future to investigate ownership of the funeral home that serves the community before the funeral is needed.

Know your funeral director and ask direct questions. Remember, there is always someone out there ready to take advantage of you and it has been done over the years by a few in the funeral industry. This is a time when people are most susceptible. The grieving persons will make decisions that they don't remember. If, and I keep stressing this fact, one knows their funeral director who is a member of the community, that person has a better chance of true, honest and faithful service before, during, and after the funeral.

I remember one owner who, every time a family chose a casket of minimum cost, would always ask me, "Why did you sell that? We don't sell that kind." In fact, I couldn't place the casket out where it could be seen. It was always covered and kept in the garage out of sight. He thought if it wasn't on view, no one would choose it. Other caskets would be placed in bad lighting or in a position in the display room known for not selling well. Some funeral home owners will show you a snapshot of an inexpensive casket, hoping you won't like it, thereby choosing one on display that they would rather sell.

If you do not see a casket within your budget, ask the director who is waiting on you. Cheaper caskets are available if that is what you can afford and want. Remember, all caskets do the same thing.

Other types of caskets seen in the average funeral home are solid hardwoods such as oak, maple, cherry and mahogany, to name a few. These are usually handcrafted and, in most cases, beautifully done. I have to admit they are my favorite caskets. They are solidly constructed, with the finest workmanship and, in most cases, with interiors fit for anyone. These caskets are usually in the upper-price range and should be. Much craftsmanship goes into each one.

Why have caskets of this type? The American public demands a choice. Look at all the cars on the highways. Look in the supermarket at all the different brands on the shelves. Now you must admit that we all like to have a choice. That's the American way. The same is true of caskets. Funeral directors would not have the variety if people did not want this choice. I want people to be aware of what they are buying.

Another type of casket is made of metal. There are several price levels in this class. It is possible to find some metal caskets less expensive than many of the solid hardwoods and cloth-covered types. Those are of a "poor" quality with a minimum of crafsmanship. For instance, 16-gauge metal is thicker than 20-gauge metal. Again, you get what you pay for in funeral merchandise, as in anything else. It's no different. Remember that.

Many of these caskets are sold because of their quality of metal and low price. Don't be fooled. Ask questions. Ask, "Why the difference in price? Why this color and not another?" Some colors are dull to discourage a person from buying it and to get them to look at more expensive caskets. Ask questions of yourself. Just because it is made of metal does not mean it is any better quality than a minimum wood casket.

The minimum metal casket does have a place. It has been my experience over the years that many people like the looks and "feel" of a metal casket. I believe that a person should buy what they want and not what the funeral director wishes to sell.

The high quality metal caskets are what most funeral home owners like to sell. The profit margin is greatest in the "middle-of-the-road" caskets. More of this type than any other are on view in the selection room. These are usually well made, but not always. Some casket manufacturers' quality leaves much to be desired. Many may look good, but the quality is low. The funeral director knows which ones they are.

Most metal caskets are made with a rubber gasket around the edges designed to seal out air and water. There are many of these so-called "sealer" caskets that are far from leak proof. Any honest funeral director will show those which he would not buy for this reason. There are also a few casket manufacturers who do not put out a good, dependable sealer casket. But, do not be mislead by the warranty claim against casket leakage. Manufacturers can claim anything, but deliver very little. How is one to know?

Do not for one moment think that just because a casket has a rubber gasket designed to keep out air and water that it will. I have seen caskets disinterred after one month that were full of water though they were sold as "air and water tight." Do not be afraid to ask questions if this is important to you.

In more than 35 years as a mortician, I do not have any faith at all in so-called "sealer" caskets. If you want protection from the elements, you should consider a crypt in a mausoleum or a quality vault to seal the casket within, which I will explain in a following chapter.

Another class of caskets seen in the selection room are copper and bronze. These are for those people who appreciate the quality of a semi-precious metal and can afford the cost. I have had the privilege of seeing a few of these top-quality caskets sold. A copper/bronze casket will never rust under any conditions. These "coffins" are occasionally and still, to this day, unearthed in the Middle East in excellent condition after thousands of years underground. They are truly a privilege to bury someone in, knowing they are the finest a funeral director can provide in protection from the elements.

Another line of caskets one might see are those made of stainless steel and fiberglass. These encompass a small part of casket sales. They are of high quality with high prices to match.

The ultimate, though, are the silver deposit caskets, costing many thousands of dollars. Most funeral directors have never seen one. Occasionally, a head of state or a famous entertainer will be interred in one.

Most people do not know that it is possible to make their own casket. I have seen some very nice caskets made by individuals. I think it is an opportunity for a family member to take a personal part in a loved one's burial. There is no law that requires one to buy a casket. A person can make their own and furnish it to the funeral home. That was how it was done in the past. In fact, one can buy plans for this purpose.

It is also possible to be buried in a cardboard box if that is of one's choosing. It is done. I have personally witnessed it several times. A casket does need certain specifications to meet cemetery size requirements, as do homemade wooden caskets.

Casket manufacturing began to fill a need as the nation began to grow after the Civil War. At first, community furniture dealers made burial containers. As demand increased for better caskets and for metal caskets with plush interiors, they soon were unable to meet the demand. Thus, the casket manufacturer evolved. Today, large factories manufacture caskets that are shipped throughout the country and the world.

The best advice I could give anyone would be to make any funeral arrangements well in advance of need. It is much easier to make an intelligent decision before being forced to do so. Ask questions! Any honest mortician does not mind questions. If one gets evasive answers, then look for another funeral director, even if it means going to the next nearest town. You will not be turned down. I guarantee it. It's much easier and less expensive to choose a funeral director before one is needed. If one's funeral director is responsible, he will offer families a full range of caskets from which to choose. Expensive caskets should only be a choice if the family wishes to have it that way.

Chapter 4

Cremation, Then What?

Often I am asked the following: What about cremation? Can we still have a funeral service? What happens when a person is cremated? What can be done with the cremains (ashes) after cremation?

Cremation is just another form of final disposition. Cremation speeds the time from when a person dies until he or she returns back to the earth in a natural state.

Complete funeral services can be held to honor the person's life. Viewing and chapel services can be held before cremation takes place. The deceased can be present at the service, in a casket, if the family so chooses. Or, viewing can be held in a separate room, without a casket, and services held in the chapel or elsewhere.

When a body is taken to the crematory, it is usually in a casket or some type of container for handling purposes. Cardboard boxes are quite common and low cost.

Once there, the container with the body is placed inside the "retort." It looks very much like an oven. The sides, top and bottom are lined with firebricks similar to those in a fireplace.

Most modern-day crematories are fueled by natural gas and are located in a cemetery. They handle cremations for funeral homes in that area. Some individual funeral homes operate crematories for their own use.

The cremation process takes three to four hours, depending on the size of the body. The process incinerates all soft tissue and leaves only bones and teeth. This is swept out and crushed, then ground or processed to make the remains small enough to be placed in an urn.

There are many different kinds of urns available through the funeral director or cemetery. They range from a thin sheet bronze "box" or solid bronze to marble, granite, fiberglass or wood. Some temporary urns, of plastic or cardboard, are available in most states. There are even "double" urns available so the cremains of two can be placed in the same urn.

From that point, the remains are returned to the funeral director for placement according to family instructions.

After cremation, there are a number of options available for disposition of the ashes, depending upon the laws in a particular state. Most common is burial in a cemetery. The majority of cemeteries allow an existing grave to be used where the ashes can be placed on top of a previous burial or under the headstone.

Also, most cemeteries have a columbarium where ashes can be placed within a niche. Some niches have glass fronts where the urn is visible inside. The urn is engraved with the deceased's name and dates which will be read through the glass. Granite/marble or bronze-faced niches have the name and dates engraved on the outside, and the ashes are placed in the wall behind the engraving.

Laws allowing, ashes may be scattered within the cemetery grounds such as in a rose garden or other acceptable area. Some states allow scattering over public lands and water. Organized ceremonies can take place at that time when there is the choice. The ceremonies can be observed on land, from a boat, or from an airplane when scattering by air.

The funeral director can make the arrangements or put a family in touch with the necessary people to carry out their wishes. Ashes may be taken home in most states.

Cremation societies offer services to families. Some societies leave much to be desired, while others offer complete and professional services. If people could see the unprofessional personnel of some societies, their low regard for the deceased and the manner in which they conduct business, potential clients would not employ a cremation service without first investigating it through the Better Business Bureau or such agencies.

Ask several nurses, off the record, at your local hospital/nursing home to tell you of their observation of cremation societies' personnel versus the local funeral home removal personnel. One will find a high degree of professionalism associated with the local funeral home as opposed to cremation societies in general.

Usually a cremation society offers just cremation and nothing more. They make the removal, do the paper work, cremate and arrange for final disposition as per one's wishes. Most of the time, the local funeral director can provide the same service at the same cost or less and with professional people.

Don't be misled by advertisements of low cremation cost. Beware that when a person engages a cremation society, they sometimes pay more than if they used their local funeral home.

Cremation societies may advertise low prices. But when the customer makes arrangements, there may be add-on costs for other services the society provides because the customer doesn't know how to handle it. Make arrangements in advance of need, if possible, and be sure they are complete and understood.

Many people belong to a cremation society with a membership fee paid in advance. But that does not mean that all arrangements are completed or paid for. People have found that their membership fee was of no benefit. Most often, it does not make a difference whether or not one belongs. The price is the same to everyone.

You frequently will hear, "We are running out of space for cemeteries." If you have ever flown over any part of the world, how many cemeteries could you see below? None, probably! Lack of space is not a reason to choose cremation. That is just a scare tactic.

Cremation is being used by county welfare officials in some areas of the United States when social services are called upon for help. These provide for immediate cremation with no services unless made by the family on their own and at their own expense.

Choose cremation only if it is your desire to do so. It is a safe and clean way of disposition and has been practiced for thousands of years in other parts of the world.

You can be present during the actual cremation process if you so wish and have the next of kin's permission. If a funeral director tells you it's not possible for you to witness the actual cremation, walk out without saying another word and go to another funeral home. When you are told that you are not able to witness the cremation, it usually means the crematory has something to hide.

Chapter 5

What Happens At The Cemetery Before You Get There And After You Leave?

I am not going to describe the many thousands of country cemeteries that are taken care of by a board of directors and the community. Most are well cared for while others are left abandoned and forgotten. I will talk about the large ones that are perfectly landscaped with manicured lawns and gardens, the cemeteries with large statues and magnificent buildings with expensive marble floors, those that are out to make a profit from people.

A cemetery can be as restful and beautiful a place as one would ever want for their loved one's final resting place. Most are quite pleasant.

What happens in cemeteries that people are not aware of? What kind of problems could there possibly be? Unfortunately, there are plenty of problems in managing and operating a cemetery.

For instance, burial in the wrong lot is common. Be sure that when a loved one is put to rest that he or she is in the grave site you purchased. And, if a person owns more than one grave for future use, make sure one knows exactly where it is. In record-keeping, things can be registered incorrectly. People make mistakes. Nothing is more upsetting than to discover the grave, crypt or niche next to Mom or Dad has been sold to someone else.

Sunken graves are common because of soil settling after the burial is completed. This happens because the grave was not properly filled and the soil tamped. After a rain or irrigation, the soil will settle. A word to the cemetery office will usually correct the problem.

Don't expect flowers to remain on the grave for any extended period. Nothing looks worse than wilted or dried up flowers on a grave unless it's plastic flowers. Plastic has a phony look and after a few days in the sun those flowers look even worse. The same goes for windmills or any other type of decorations people try to put on graves. Many cemeteries have rules prohibiting such things. The cemetery will remove flowers at the next mowing, in most cases, or at a given time interval after a holiday.

Leaving potted plants at a grave is acceptable, but be aware that some people will scout cemeteries for potted plants to sell at flea markets. That sounds cold, but I have seen and caught numerous people doing this.

Some cemeteries will let one reserve a space for a short time until arrangements can be made to purchase it. But, do not think of it as indefinite. It's up to the customer to contact the cemetery if he wants additional lots, usually within 30 to 90 days.

When making cemetery arrangements, know the difference between a grave liner and a grave vault.

A grave liner is usually made of concrete without a bottom. It only keeps the grave from caving in when the casket deteriorates and collapses in later years. For example, this could happen in country cemeteries with sunken areas where a grave liner is not required. Grave liners keep the long term cost of care lower by eliminating labor costs to refill the grave and reseed with grass.

A grave vault is a receptacle in which the casket is sealed and protected from the surrounding environment. There are many manufacturers of burial vaults in every major city in the United States. One can get simple concrete vaults with an asphalt seal around the lid—to those lined completely with stainless steel and copper. Remember, a liner is usually a cemetery requirement for the benefit of the cemetery. It does not protect the casket from the elements.

Also, the cemetery may ask about a grave marker or headstone to be placed over the grave. When purchasing one, make sure that the engraving is correct, and that the headstone is placed on the right burial plot. The gravesite one has been visiting may not be where the loved one is actually buried. It's easy for cemetery personnel to make a mistake when trying to locate a particular grave and place a marker on it. Check it out against the deed and have cemetery personnel prove that it is the correct place.

If a grave digger is not careful, he can get a grave off center or even in the wrong row. Therefore, the next burial will be off center and so on. Be aware of this problem.

People have always heard of being buried under six feet of ground. Think again. Most cemeteries only have about eighteen inches of earth over the top of the burial receptacle. Some are known to have even less. There is pending legislation in some states to require a minimum amount of soil covering a grave.

The only way one can be buried six feet under is if one is at the bottom of a multiple burial. That is, where several are buried in the same grave, one on top of the other. I have known some cemeteries to bury three deep, one on top of the other.

Why don't cemetery personnel lower the casket before all mourners have left? It's because they do not want people there to watch what they do. It makes them nervous for the public to be aware of some of the problems I have mentioned earlier. Cemetery personnel like to be notified in advance so as to avoid any embarrassment. Caskets are dropped, stood upon, pushed and even broken sometimes when lowered into the grave. I would have a family member or friend of the family stay behind to observe the interment.

Some cemeteries allow raised markers in certain areas. But, more common today are park-like settings where all markers are flat. Quite often the cemetery will allow memorial benches or statues placed in certain areas in memory of a loved one. Sometimes, only certain types of granite or bronze markers are allowed. Check this out before purchasing a marker so that you will not be disappointed when the time comes to place one.

Most modern day cemeteries have an endowment care fund in which a percentage of the grave's purchase price is deposited into a special trust account. That portion of money can never be touched or removed, in most states. Only the interest income can be used for cemetery upkeep. This insures that the cemetery will always have income to care for upkeep after it is filled to capacity.

Ask for a disclosure of endowment funds to see that it is being spent on cemetery improvement projects. If the cemetery is not accomodating, write or call your state cemetery board for help.

Most cemeteries sell their own headstones within the gates as a matter of convenience to lot owners. This makes sense to make all the arrangements within one place. People have the right to go to a private monument dealer or funeral home where they can usually get a better price.

The cemetery does have the right to dictate the size and types of headstones allowed in certain sections. Remember this when choosing a gravesite in advance of need. One may not like the type of marker required in a certain area and may want to select elsewhere in that cemetery or go to a different cemetery.

Present-day trends are to have a cemetery-mortuary-crematory combination all in one place. In this type of facility, the family can make all the arrangements there for final disposition. This really makes good sense and is practical for the public.

It is not required to use the funeral home in the cemetery. One also can use the mortuary within the cemetery grounds and go to an outside cemetery elsewhere in the community. Each part of such a combination is operated separately, one from the other, and can be used individually without being required to use the other divisions.

If one wants the ultimate in protection, consider a crypt in a mausoleum. A crypt is a place of burial inside a wall in a building. Mausoleums are traditionally made of concrete with varying heights to individual crypts. Tiers of six high are common. The lower down the crypt, the more expensive. The most expensive are at eye level.

This is the most expensive type of cemetery property because of high costs and continued maintenance over the years. There is less chance of water being a reason for concern. Inspect the mausoleum before deciding to buy. During rainy seasons, I have seen water streaming from crypts. A building is only as good as its roof.

Outside crypts, also called garden crypts, are becoming popular. Instead of being inside a building, the crypts are all on the outside facing outward where one can walk around the building. There is no "inside" to the building.

Chapter 6

The Traditional Funeral Service

Most people are familiar with the traditional funeral. A person dies, they're embalmed and dressed. A time of viewing and visiting is set aside, usually the night before the service. The service is then held, customarily in the funeral home chapel, a lodge, hall or at a local church the person may have belonged to or attended. All predictable and functional for the most part.

This was how our grandparents and parents usually handled funerals. And, for many of us today, it is the way most will handle them. Yet many people have different ideas on what they want for loved ones and for themselves.

In one form or another, funeral services are important in many different ways to people. The "traditional" funeral as we know it is the most beneficial therapy that we can bestow upon ourselves.

Why do you suppose we go to such lengths to recover a person who may be lost at sea, in the wilderness, on a snow covered mountain or wherever? It is because of our need to know for sure that the person is "gone." We have heard ourselves say, "I can't believe he or she is really dead. I just talked to him or her the other day."

The time immediately after we first learn of a friend or loved one's death is often a time of confusion and bewilderment — a time when some people suffer from shock. It's a time when the reality of life's shortness hits home. It's a painful time to endure, and it's important that we deal with our feelings in a manner beneficial for healing.

A funeral or time of acknowledgment does exactly that. It gives family and friends a chance to acknowledge and accept the fact that a person's life has ended on this earth. It's a time of gathering for friends and relatives to meet and talk about their loss and share their feelings.

Every individual has his or her own particular way of dealing with loss. How that is done is important to our future well-being.

If a person has lived any kind of a life, why not remember it and give it a closing chapter?

Otherwise, why not just get rid of those who die in any manner regardless of how it's done?

The answer is obvious. We care! We care about those we know, and we have respect for the survivors. We pay our respects because we care about them. It's that simple.

So, a traditional funeral is important in this country today. It gives an opportunity for friends, neighbors and members of the community the chance to express concern.

There are exceptions to this in some areas of the United States. For instance, in Marin County, California, in a majority of deaths, there are what is referred to as "Direct Cremations." It's what some professionals refer to as "garbage service." "Box and burn." I dealt with this subject in a previous chapter.

I have found the country's rural areas are definite in the traditional funeral. I contribute that to the fact that country people depend on one another. When a neighbor needs help in any way, or when one dies, they all come together to offer support and to receive support in return. It's a time of talking; and sharing emotions, thoughts and experiences. It is almost the complete opposite in large metropolitan areas.

No one likes to talk about death, but a funeral gives everyone the opportunity to deal with one's death and to express one's self. When one can talk about their feelings on any subject that may be painful, almost always they will feel better.

Whether accidents, suicides, homicides or natural deaths, we all need a chance to talk about it in order to go on with our lives. A funeral service helps us to adjust.

Trying to avoid the fact that someone close to you has died only hurts yourself. Denial only prolongs the acceptance that needs to come. There is no time limit in accepting. It can take days, weeks, months and even years.

Some people never come to that place of acceptance in the loss of a loved one. That is why it's wise to deal with it as soon as possible. It's a difficult time and measured in different ways for each of us.

Funerals, who needs them? I don't want any in my family. No normal person enjoys going to funerals, even myself, a professional funeral director all these years. When the day comes to a close, and I reflect on the day's events, it takes some time to adjust to "normal."

I, too, spent many months grieving over the loss of a loved one. No two of us are alike, and we need to be patient with one another at such a difficult time. Give space and acceptance to those who need it, even when it does not agree with your own philosophy. Would you want any less for yourself?

To purposely stay away from a funeral hurts only oneself. It will only take longer, if ever, to recover from the loss.

Remember, a funeral can be a lot of different things besides the "traditional" type of service. It can be a time of silence beside a stream in the mountains, or at the seashore, or in the backyard. It can be several close friends talking and sharing their thoughts of the deceased. It can be a gathering at the funeral home, one's own home, the office or workplace or on a mountaintop. It really doesn't matter, as long as a person finds a way to put an end to his or her loss.

If one is a part of a family who chooses an untraditional type of service, why not out of respect and to help yourself, honor that person? People will never be sorry for attending a service. However, they may be sorry for the rest of their lives if they do not attend.

Chapter 7

What Does The Coroner Do?

The coroner or medical examiner is called when death occurs in an accident or homicide or if there is an unattended death.

The coroner is called in on all nursing home care facility deaths in some states because of the poor quality of care plaguing the "nursing home" care industry. They are called to hospital emergency rooms when the deceased was admitted less than 24 hours prior to death or if a patient dies of injuries from any cause known or unknown. They are also called in when someone who has not been under a doctor's care dies.

The coroner determines the cause of death from medical history and from family and neighbors, if information is available. Or, he can order an autopsy to determine the cause. It is here that there is much controversy.

When should an autopsy be ordered? In some cities and counties, every death the coroner investigates is autopsied. This is a stupid and cruel misuse of authority. It is my opinion from more than 35 years experience that this is done only to spend public money and to provide an extra income for the pathologist (who may be the coroner as well). Autopsies may be performed on a case-by-case fee, amounting to hundreds and hundreds of dollars. The cause of death is so obviuos most of the time that a child could recognize it but, time after time, an autopsy will be ordered.

There are times when an autopsy is the only answer to determine cause of death. I would want one done on myself to determine cause of death for my family's peace of mind if there were no visible reasons. Also, there are times when an autopsy can benefit medical science. That may not always be the case. Hospital personnel try to get autopsy permission on every person who dies. It's good for their ratings.

If a person has been under a doctor's care for some time, however, an autopsy should never be required. If one's doctor does not know the cause of death after treating the person, then I believe that the person may have had the wrong doctor. The family should tell the doctor so when he or the hospital nurses request an autopsy.

I have encountered doctors who refused to sign a death certificate because they did not know the cause of death for a person who had been under their care for some time. Avoid these doctors like the plague. What does this tell you about their medical care and knowledge?

What happens in an autopsy? It depends on the pathologist performing the procedure and the institution for which he works.

In most autopsies, every organ is removed and inspected for disease or injury. Usually a tissue sample is taken along with blood and other fluid samples for further study in the laboratory.

At some institutions, everything is removed from the body, including the brain. All that is left is a shell. By the time the funeral director receives the remains, he must attempt to prepare the body for viewing, covering pathologist mistakes and "slips" with the scalpel.

It is my opinion that these types of pathologists and health care facilities are nothing but "meat shops." There is no respect for the person's dignity. After all, it's not their worry as far as they are concerned. Any funeral director can tell you, off the record, which pathologists, coroners and hospitals fall into this category. This is one case I believe the movies and television have stereotyped correctly.

There are a few thoughtful pathologists who treat all bodies with respect and consider what they are doing.

Think of that when a loved one dies, and you are asked to consent to an autopsy for the "benefit of mankind." That is so much nonsense. Hospitals are rated on how many autopsies they get consent for with signed forms. Always check with the funeral director before signing an autopsy consent form no matter who is encouraging you to do so. Tell your doctor before that time arises that you do or do not want an autopsy.

Another type of consent form most hospitals try to get signed is for organ donation. Consider carefully before giving unlimited authority for this. When given permission, I have seen them sweep in like vultures. They remove all organs being used to transplant these days. That fact is not bad in itself. It's the way in which it is done to which I object. No respect at all! It is common to remove a large portion of skin, bones, the inner ears and any other parts they may want.

There is no doubt in my mind that this is a worthwhile cause. But, I have seen so many remains totally mutilated that I personally would never give consent on a family member of mine. The body is almost without form and, if it weren't for the work of the funeral director/embalmer, it would not be viewable for families who wish to do so.

The public is not aware of the condition of the body after organ removal or many would not grant permission. And, the funeral director is not going to add to the family's grief at this time.

I might give consent for a limited donation authorization if I were acquainted with the person or persons performing the surgery to remove the organs. I would never give them unlimited consent organ donation.

The best way to find out about organ donor banks in your area is to ask your funeral director. He has first-hand knowledge of their practices and procedures.

Demand your right to know in detail or *do not* give permission. Then, follow up through your funeral director. Do not ask the doctor. One is not likely to get a straight-forward answer on the real facts. They protect their own.

Chapter 8

Clergy, Friend Or Foe?

Clergy selection could quite possibly be one of the most important decisions that a family can make. The entire funeral service hinges around this person. The decision should be made with a great deal of consideration.

The family should ask a member of the clergy with whom they are comfortable. It doesn't have to be the pastor of one's particular church. In fact, sometimes that is probably the worst choice one could make. I say this because some pastors do not have the training to know the best way to conduct a funeral or memorial service or how to be of help to the families they serve. Other pastors may be so set in their own ways that they do not have the consideration of the family in mind.

A few of the "traditional" pastors couldn't care less about what the family wants or needs. Some pastors have a set way of conducting funerals that is the same for every family they serve. Each family in need of a funeral is unique. Each family needs to be considered on its own terms, but it is next to impossible to get this through to some pastors.

There are ministers who do have the survivors' interest at heart. The clergy should ask every family how it would like the funeral service to be conducted. Clergy should know the history, likes, dislikes, humorous events in the deceased's life and, of course, his or her religious beliefs. Remember, a funeral service is for the living. A service is held because a life has ended, and that life is one that is worth remembering. How cold this world would be if, when a person dies, we would just continue to go on as if if he or she had never lived.

That is why we record history in books—so it won't be forgotten. It's true that some people would just as soon forget that a person has died, but this is a means of rationalization and denial. They are not facing up to reality. The time will come later when they will have to face the loss.

There is a certain degree of "ceremony" in all religious services. It is important to have a plan of order in carrying out ones' wishes. When a life is memorialized it is important that it be carried out with dignity. For the most part, most clergy do, but tell them what is wanted and expected in arranging a funeral for a loved one.

Another thing to consider is that anyone can conduct a funeral or memorial service. It does not have to be a member of the clergy. In every community, there are excellent veterans' organizations to help. These veterans will assist because a comrade has fallen. They do not ask or expect to be paid for their services. But a gratuity is appreciated for the benefit of the Post.

They usually have a chaplain, honor guard, a firing squad and two veterans to fold the flag (if one covers the casket) and present it to the next of kin. They will conduct an entire service from beginning to end.

Other service organizations in your area that will do the same are: Masonic Lodge; Order of Eastern Star; Elks Lodge; Moose Lodge; Odd Fellows Lodge; and many other associations.

One's funeral director, with a little information, can advise on what and whom would best present a meaningful funeral service.

I offer a little advice to any clergy who may be reading this: remember whom you are serving. It's a man or woman, not yourself. A funeral service is not the time or place to preach a fire and brimstone message. Just because there is a captive audience, don't exploit it for your own purposes. Remember, you are dealing with aching hearts and, in most cases, these people will leave with hard feelings toward you.

I have had families ask to stop a funeral service right in the middle of a message, because the minister was preaching a conversion message instead of a funeral service in honor of the deceased.

It is so difficult to get through to some ministers that they are there to serve, not to serve themselves. Clergy are there to give instruction, faith, hope, and a reason to keep looking forward and not put people on a guilt trip, which many clergy try to do.

A funeral service should never go more than 30 to 45 minutes. In most cases, 20 minutes is sufficient. At a graveside service where everyone is standing, 10 to 15 minutes at the most is adequate.

The clergy should discuss the life of the deceased. People attend a funeral service because they have a personal connection to the deceased, *not* because of the officiant and his life!

Clergy should almost never be present when arrangements are made. All too often they will only be thinking of their own wants and not the family's. When the minister is present, the family may feel obligated to give in to his or her wishes.

When it comes to a member of the minister's own family, it's completely different. For instance, a member of the clergy will tell the family it's not important what kind of casket to choose. A family will often pick out a casket they like. The minister will almost always have them buy a cheaper casket. But when a minister is making arrangements for one of his loved ones, I believe it's anything but that. They will almost always pick a casket in the upper-price range.

I agree that it does not make a difference what casket one chooses. I have observed clergy, though, saying one thing while doing another for themselves.

In our country's large urban areas, the clergy expect and demand that the funeral director send a limousine to his or her door. If the director is unable or not willing to do this, then that director is not likely to be recommended. Also, at holidays and special occasions, the funeral director who sends the nicest gifts get the most recommendations from certain clergy. This sounds like a horrible practice, but it happens more than most people know.

My advice to all clergy is to find out from families what makes them feel uncomfortable about funerals. And then, respect it. Most families are not rejecting funerals, just the style. There are many ways to help families, without demanding one's own standards.

Keep the funeral simple, more of a gathering of family and friends. The service should be a celebration of a life that has been lived. The funeral ceremony gives the family an avenue to express grief and to receive support from family and friends.

It is customary to give a gratuity to the person conducting the service. The funeral director will do this to avoid any embarrassment to the family. He will advise on what is normal for the area.

There are a few clergy who will not accept money for funerals. I once asked why and was told, "The church pays me a salary to minister to the needs of the members and this is part of that ministry."

That was an exception. Most often, gratuities are an important part of their salary. I highly recommend it be done through the funeral director or the family, if members are close to the minister.

Chapter 9

Funeral Etiquette

If one chooses to have a traditional funeral, or to attend one, *be on time*. There is nothing so rude as being late to a funeral. When arriving late, one interrupts the proceedings. By being late one indicates that they really didn't care enough to leave ten minutes earlier. If a person cannot be on time, why bother to go at all?

When guests enter the door for services, a funeral director is usually handing out memorial folders or prayer cards and directing them to a memorial book. Sign it and proceed to the seating area or at least move away from the memorial book.

Do not stand in the way of others who are waiting to sign the book, especially at a graveside service. Move a little distance away to allow room for others. Do not stand around and tell jokes and laugh as if you were at a social gathering.

You may ask, "Why are you saying this? Does this really happen?" You bet your life it does, at almost every service. The time to visit is after the service is over.

A funeral home is no place to bring food and beverage of any kind. It shows a great deal of disrespect to the decedent, and a lack of manners. Do not eat or drink inside a funeral home, whether you are there for making arrangements, visiting or attending the funeral itself. Some funeral homes have a reception area set aside for this. Ask!

Children should always be allowed to attend services if they want to. And, do not prohibit children the opportunity to express their grief. Some children feel better if they can give a gift or something of their own that is personal. It might be a drawing or a note expressing their love. This type of behavior should be encouraged.

Answer any questions a child may have. Do not put them aside or dismiss their questions as unimportant. Answering their questions gives children the feeling of belonging. In most cases, young children handle their feelings far better than adults. Children usually do not have hangups. Adults like to hold their true emotions in and, in doing so, recovery takes longer.

Speaking of children at funerals, leave babies at home or sit where you can slip out if they become fussy. I have witnessed babies at funerals hundreds of times, and mothers and fathers often sit like bumps on a log while the baby cries and fusses. If it is a family member, that's a different story. Even families will leave the very young at home most of the time for this reason. As a friend, should we do any less?

How does one dress when attending a funeral? Why not wear your best clothes? You don't have to wear black, but if you feel that black would be most appropriate and would express your sorrow, then do so.

The area of the country where the funeral is held makes a difference. In New York city, the dress is going to be quite different than in Desert Hot Springs, California. We're talking of two entirely diverse cultures. The dress at a Hell's Angel funeral will differ from that of the local bank president in most cases. But, wear what is comfortable. I would advise everyone to have the decency to be modest in dress.

At the end of a service, do not force your way out, opposite of where the director is dismissing guests. One does not have to go by the casket and view it if they don't want to. In most funeral homes, one can choose to pass by without even looking. Guests are dismissed in a certain direction so the family will be able to see them. When they go out the "back" the family never gets the chance to see those guests. It is a source of great comfort to be able to see who is attending.

If there is to be a procession to the cemetery, have the courtesy to follow behind the hearse and family cars. Do not rush out to the cemetery before everyone else. You may cause problems by parking in areas where the hearse and family vehicles need to park. It's rude to conduct oneself in this manner.

Follow in the procession and stay close to the car in front. If you lag behind, not paying attention, other drivers on the road do not know that you are part of the funeral procession. They may proceed themselves, making a break and stopping the procession at that point.

If you see a funeral procession on the road, think for a moment. If *you* were part of the procession, how would you want other drivers to behave? Do not try to break through at any opening. (And, sorry ladies, you can be the most impatient when it comes to allowing funeral processions to pass.) Check the cars that are following to see if the lights are on. Remember, too, that some people forget to turn their vehicle lights on, so check a couple of cars behind as to their status.

When arriving at the cemetery, follow the car in front and the directions of cemetery personnel handling traffic. Most of all, show patience and courtesy to any funeral procession.

After graveside services have ended and guests are dismissed, approach the family and greet them. If you don't know what to say, just say "I'm sorry." People will appreciate it. You don't have to say anything. It's just as difficult for the family to know what to say, too. A person's presence says it all.

If there is a gathering afterwards, try to attend, if at all possible. It's a time of sharing and support for friends and family.

Don't forget the family in the days that follow. They need support most at that time. Take food, visit, offer to mow the lawn or whatever. Ask them to go shopping with you. Don't be afraid to talk about the funeral and related events. Being supportive is what is needed most. It's a terrible experience to feel that one is suddenly alone and nobody cares.

What kind of music is acceptable at a funeral service? Choose music that the deceased enjoyed.

Remember, this is a celebration of the deceased's life! It's a time of remembrance of his or her life. It should, to some extent, be music one could associate with that person.

It could be a combination of different types of music — some popular modern music and some favorite religious hymns they may have liked. Do not think that a funeral has to have all religious or deep, dark, gloomy music. Make it representative of the person's life.

Musicians or vocalists should be given a gratuity in all cases. If the musician wants to return it, then so be it.

What if one is asked to be a pallbearer? What are the duties? First of all, pallbearers can be family members, male or female, or friends of the deceased and family. Pallbearers must be on time, at least fifteen minutes before the service is to start. If there are questions, call the funeral director. And wear appropriate clothing.

It's an honor to be asked to be a pallbearer. Wear your best clothing, whatever it may be. It doesn't matter. One is asked because the immediate family thinks and feels that the deceased would want them to be there.

Pallbearers are not given a gratuity for their part in the service.

When they get to the place of services, pallbearers should announce who they are as soon as possible. Usually, the funeral directors have a place where pallbearers are to be seated while waiting for others to arrive. At that time, instruction will be given regarding duties.

"Thank you" notes are usually furnished to the family for acknowledging flowers and cards sent. If you don't receive a thank you note, don't be concerned. It's just too difficult for some people to sit down and go through the grief of writing to the many friends who remembered them in this way.

Should one send flowers when "In lieu of flowers" is used in the newspaper obituary? If that is the best way for you to express yourself, flowers will be accepted.

"In lieu of flowers," is a term dreaded by florists for obvious reasons. Check the local newspaper to see if it reads that way, designating a particular charity. Some families would rather that you contribute to a particular charity. You may follow your own wishes. Flowers will always have a place at funerals.

Ordering flowers can be a shot in the dark most of the time unless you know from first-hand experience the florists in the area. You never know what you are getting when ordering over the telephone in a distant city. When I need flowers in a distant city, I ask a funeral director in that city to suggest three florists. Then, I choose the first of the three names. One thing is certain, a funeral director will know the best florist. We see so many thousands of arrangements, potted plants, sprays and so on every year that we can tell from a distance, in an instant, which florist makes which arrangements without seeing the card.

As to what kind of flowers to send, that is entirely up to you. Potted plants will stay around awhile and can be taken home after the services. But, there are times when an arrangement says exactly what you want it to say.

I can say nothing good about plastic flowers on graves. After a few days, they look terrible and phony. Which they are! Keep the plastic flowers at home. They look better there.

Another request may be donations to a trust fund set up in the deceased's memory for worthy causes in the community. These can be for community centers, schools, sport programs, etc. Most often, the family will receive an acknowledgment of your contribution in the mail from whichever organization received it. I have found that it is always best to choose a local charity group in your area. Let the donation help in your own community. All national groups are worthy, but one might as well support people at home rather than in another city.

Chapter 10

Owner/ Employee Relationship

Funeral home owners have had control over conditions for many years. And they are still trying in every conceivable manner to continue that practice.

The profession has been surrounded in mystery. It was "unprofessional" to disclose what transpired in the funeral home behind closed doors. Owners actually operate under a veil of secrecy. One rarely receives a straight, honest answer regarding anything to do with the business under the guise that it "isn't ethical". That's baloney. They do not want anyone to have the chance to criticize their work.

Most employees are afraid to say anything under the threat of dismissal if they say something the owners don't agree with. I believe that the public has the right to know what goes on in the funeral business, just as a person does in any other business.

During the 1960's, several books were written by nonprofessionals about funeral services. I read some of those books and I must admit that truths were revealed. Most of the information, however, contained a variety of errors and outright lies written by authors who had little knowledge of the subject. I believe that they wanted to make the reporting spectacular in order to sell a lot of copies. That's the American way. Make money!

Of course, funeral homes are in business to make money. If they did not make money, the service would be so poor that one would be afraid to use it, or they would simply go out of business.

It is a fact that some funeral homes are out to make as much profit from customers as possible. Believe me, after more than three decades in this business, I know that to be a fact. At the same time, I know of many honest, hardworking funeral home owners who are providing a valuable service to their community. But they are rare. (I have had the good fortune to have worked for such an employer. That is why I decided to write this account of the good and bad in funeral service).

I regret what I have to say about this profession which I love. But I feel it is impoortant to share my experience to help others. The funeral industry is a closed system to the general public.

If you have the resources to own a funeral home, it's a pretty good life. But, if you are just an ordinary working man, like I have been for many years, it's a different story.

The average working funeral home employee is at the bottom of the salary scale, considering the amount of time that is required of him or her. The profits all go to the owner, who keeps the employee pay scale as low as possible. It has been my experience that owners and managers check with one another to keep salaries at a minimum throughout the country.

A fully-qualified employee makes less than an electrician, plumber, sanitary worker, a registered nurse or truck driver, just to name a few.

The average funeral director/embalmer in the United States serves two years apprenticeship and graduates from a two-year program of mortuary science. That is four years of training in most states. Some states require a bachelor of science degree.

To be a director in most funeral homes one must be willing to work weekends and be on call 24 hours or not work at all. In most cases, there is no compensation for being on call 24 hours at a time.

If one is lucky, he or she might have a "compassionate" employer who will, out of the goodness of his heart, pay an employee time and a half for actual time working. For instance, say it is 2 a.m. and the telephone rings with a call from the local hospital, nursing home, coroner's office or a family residence informing you that a person has died. In most cases, you will have to come right away to remove the deceased no matter where it may be.

You drag yourself out of bed, get dressed , go into the funeral home and load a cot into the removal vehicle. You go to the place of death, make the removal back to the funeral home and then go back home to await the next call and try to sleep, if possible. Then, at 8 a.m., one is expected to be freshand ready to put in a full day's work.

If you are paid for one hour of overtime, you consider yourself lucky. At most funeral homes, overtime is expected without any compensation. Not many owners care about fair labor laws but only how much they can get you to work for free.

Is the owner concerned? Not likely, in most cases. There are rare exceptions. When any employee "burns out," the employer asks, "Who's next?" And they complain, "Isn't it a shame that there isn't any good help out there!"

Morticians have tried to organize many times but, by use of scare tactics, owners have prevented them from doing so. Unions have such a bad image that it has been a lost cause in most cities and states.

It is difficult to find many women employees or owners, because they have been shut out of the profession. Women are becoming more visible in the field because of their attributes. Today, more women own funeral homes.

Women make good directors because of their compassion and understanding in most cases. Many times a woman can console a widow better than a man without raising eyebrows, especially in the post-care time after the funeral. Also, women usually provide a point of view entirely different from a man's. Women have the ability to put on a nice finishing touch.

Chapter 11

Paperwork
And
Mechanics

Funerals involve a mountain of paperwork. The public is unaware of how funeral homes, cemeteries, or crematories operate. In a funeral home, paperwork begins when the telephone rings.

As soon as a director picks up the telephone, he or she has a pencil in hand, ready to take notes. From there, it's a constant string of documents: hospital release forms; death certificates; burial permits; request forms for certified copies of death certificates; cremation authorization forms; crematory report forms; memorial folders; clergy records; Social Security reports; insurance claims forms; Veterans Administration benefit forms; V.A. flag forms, marker forms, life insurance forms; contracts; arrangement forms; ledgers to be made for bookkeeping; and all of the bookkeeping procedure supply order forms!

The list goes on and on. These are just a few of the forms and paperwork that need to be done every day for each family the funeral director serves. This is what takes most of the time and labor to arrange a funeral and to carry it out.

So far, we have just talked about office work. There are many mechanical conveyances that need maintenance, such as the removal vehicles. This is usually a station wagon or a van. There are family cars to be looked after and kept clean and in good working order.

In some cities, the clergy demand and expect a limousine to pick them up. There is also the coach (hearse) and a van for taking the flowers from the church or funeral home to the cemetery. On a "normal" funeral, from the time the telephone rings until the services are completed, it takes an average of six different vehicles. All of these need to be attended to and kept ready to go 24 hours a day.

Can you imagine the cost in upkeep, gasoline and insurance? It's no small matter. Think of this the next time you need a funeral director who must be ready whether or not all of his services are used.

Other equipment that people don't think about are items such as removal cots. Several are needed and are quite expensive. Funeral home expenses also include laundry service, yard and lawn service, as well as all the normal building upkeep during the winter and summer, and insurance. Most people do not know of these expenses when they think about a funeral. When one pays for the professional services of a funeral director, there are all these expenses plus many more not mentioned.

Chapter 12

Insurance, Social Security, And Veterans Benefits

Usually, there is much information and little understanding about survivors' benefits. The belief that someone will take care of it at the time is not always the way it turns out.

Many times insurance goes unclaimed just because no one is aware that insurance policies even exist. Or, one family member will think that someone else is taking care of it. All family members should know what to do in the event of a death. They should know where all valuable papers, such as insurance policies, are kept and who the beneficiaries are.

Papers should be kept up to date. Do not keep them in your safe deposit box at the bank. It might be impossible to remove the papers after the death of the box holder for some time, depending on the rules of your bank.

If one beneficiary dies before the other then the policy should be changed. It's a simple matter to handle. It can be a big problem later if ignored.

It has been my experience that it is best to put one person in charge of affairs, with a secondary person named in case something happens to the first designee. But having one person, whom one knows will carry out one's exact wishes with fairness, is much better than having all the children sharing in responsibilities.

Time after time, in many families, the children cannot agree with one another. This can hurt family relationships and lead to a court battle. If a family member does not like this arrangement, that's his or her problem. Therefore, put one person in charge of final arrangements.

A person may have purchased insurance policies earlier from a company that no longer exists. This is quite common. Insurance companies will buy one another's policies, sometimes several times over, making it difficult to track down. I speak from experience. It's not impossible to do, however. We are accustomed to this type of run-around by some companies.

Keep any proof of premiums paid no matter how old. This type of evidence has paid off more than once for beneficiaries. Once you have proof of premiums paid, some companies suddenly find the policy in question and pay the claim.

Social Security has a death benefit payable only to a surviving spouse. In the past, Social Security paid a death benefit on everyone. Not any longer. Your funeral director will be knowledgeable on these matters and will help with them.

The funeral director will be able to help in most insurance matters by filling out claim forms and seeing that they get forwarded to the proper claims office. A trust officer at your bank can sometimes be helpful. Of course, an attorney who specializes in estates would be an excellent choice for advice.

There are some benefits if one is a veteran. Most communities have V.A. service officers who can advise best on benefits due to one's survivors.

Chapter 13

Humor In A Funeral Home?

Morticians are human. Most are dedicated to their career, but that does not mean we go around with a look of doom and gloom on our faces.

There are times when we must be as serious as one can imagine. But, we are just like any other group of people working together. We have our light moments among ourselves. And, we're accustomed to laughing at ourselves.

There are many one-liners about what we do. For instance, "We're the last ones in town to let you down"; "Business is picking up"; "Business has been dead lately"; "People are dying to see me"; "It's the only time you can legally get laid in public." The jokes go on and on.

Things that are funny to us are not necessarily funny to someone else. There was the time I was making a removal out in the Southern California desert. It was a home death, and a deputy sheriff was there.

I went into the house to see what equipment was needed to make the removal, then I left. I must have forgotten something. I returned to the room and came up behind a deputy standing in the doorway. He did not hear me, so I touched him on the arm. He actually jumped six inches. He must have been a rookie and thought someone from underground reached up and was attempting to pull him down. After 30 years, I still smile at that.

Another time, I had a young apprentice with me at a graveside service. We were placing the casket on the grave when he decided to step right into the middle of the site, not thinking that there was a grave under the greens. He fell into the grave. That is something a lay person might do.

Another time I took the wrong route to the cemetery, thinking I was going to another one. This was not funny to me, but amused my associates and the family who told me the deceased was always taking the long way home. On another occasion, I ran out of gas on the way to the cemetery. This was not funny, but it remains a source of humor to associates. The family said, "She just didn't want to go to the cemetery."

There have been other embarrassing moments, such as the time my pager went off in church. The pastor stopped to bid me farewell as everyone was chuckling.

Once an employee pretented that he was a carnival "barker" before people arrived for the funeral. He was saying, "Programs, get your programs right here." However, much to his surprise, when he turned around, someone had already arrived early for the service. This happened more than 35 years ago, and the employee still gets teased about it.

There have been times when all the employees started a "pool" on the exact time a benediction by a long-winded minister would take.

If one thing "sticks" with you in reading this book, I hope it is that funerals are for the living and in memory of the deceased. They are not for the funeral director, clergy, neighbors or friends. The final disposition should be as you want it to be. Don't accept criticism from outsiders on how they would have done it, or from other family members who are outspoken. If they wanted to help, they should have been with you when you made the arrangements.

Checklist

1. Choose a funeral director/funeral home before one is needed.
   a. Choose more than one and check them out.

2. Call for an appointment.
   a. Ask them to send you a price list before your appointment.

3. Ask for price lists.
   a. Casket prices/costs for professional services.
   b. Differences in caskets.
   c. When is embalming required?
   d. Cost of "extras," limo's, flowers, flower car, memorial book, memorial folders, thank you cards, viewing room, clergy, musicians, honorariums, etc.
   e. Provide your own clothing for deceased.
   f. Ask if you can provide your own casket. You may make your own or buy one from someone else, even another funeral director.

4. Ask about cremation.
   a. Cremation before services.
   b. Cremation after services.
   c. Cremation with no service of any kind.
   d. How are ashes disposed of?

5. Choose cemetery and purchase lots as soon as possible.
   a. Ask for a list of restrictions within the cemetery. (Different cemeteries have different rules.)
   b. What kind of markers are permitted?
   c. What kind of flowers are permitted?
   d. What about ground water? (This is a real problem in parts of every cemetery.)
   e. Ask to be shown what type of grave liner is required.
   f. Ask to see a vault and a liner.
   g. Ask for a price list of all charges.

6. Ask cemetery management if they have a mausoleum.
   a. Ask to see crypts and the total price of entombment.
   b. Ask the same questions about niches, if you choose cremation.
   c. Endowment care trust fund for the cemetery.
      (1) Are monuments and markers covered under this fund?
   d. Does the cemetery have security against vandalism?

About The Author

Clarence W. Miller was born, raised, and educated in western Oregon, where he is now retired and enjoying life. After receiving his mortuary-cemetery training at various west coast funeral homes and cemeteries, he became a general manager of major west coast mortuary-cemetery-mausoleum-crematory facilities. Clarence is licensed as a funeral director, embalmer, cemetery manager, crematory operator, cemetery grounds superintendent, and deputy coroner. He managed a wide range of funeral establishments, from small facilities in rural communities to elegant funeral homes in large cities. After working in all aspects of the funeral industry, he says, "I've enjoyed every minute of a fascinating career."

Clarence has presented talks about the funeral industry to service clubs, church groups, and schools. He has attended various seminars throughout the United States, sponsored by casket companies and motivational management clinics.

As a young boy, he learned about "The Golden Rule" (Do unto others as you would have them do unto you.) from his mother. This philosophy proved to be highly beneficial for his work in the funeral industry—an industry which has been shrouded in secrecy and half truths for many years. He openly shares his insights, experience, and knowledge in a new "behind the scenes" guide, *The Funeral Book*, to help consumers better understand the industry. He reveals how he was belittled, discriminated against, and fired from a job because of his belief in The Golden Rule. Throughout his career in funeral service, Clarence maintained his commitment to being honest and compassionate with grieving families.

(OK To Photocopy Order Form)

To order additional copies of *The Funeral Book* (ISBN 1-885003-02-1), fill out the form below and return it with payment for all orders. Thank you.

Send me _____ copies at a total cost of $_____.

$7.95 each, plus $2.50 for first book (S&H) & $0.50 each additional copy. Save on larger orders! Order 10 copies for your friends or organization for only $69.00 (Free shipping!).

Ship Books To:

Name: _____

Organization: _____

Address: _____

City: _____ State: _____ Zip: _____

Telephone: _____ Fax: _____

Order Books From The Publisher:

Robert D. Reed, Publishers
750 La Playa, Suite 647 • San Francisco, CA 94121
Telephone: 1-800-PR-GREEN

(OK To Photocopy Order Form)

To order additional copies of *The Funeral Book* (ISBN 1-885003-02-1), fill out the form below and return it with payment for all orders. Thank you.

Send me _____ copies at a total cost of $_____.

$7.95 each, plus $2.50 for first book (S&H) & $0.50 each additional copy. Save on larger orders! Order 10 copies for your friends or organization for only $69.00 (Free shipping!).

Ship Books To:

Name: _____

Organization: _____

Address: _____

City: _____ State: ____ Zip: _____

Telephone: _____ Fax: _____

Order Books From The Publisher:

Robert D. Reed, Publishers
750 La Playa, Suite 647 • San Francisco, CA 94121
Telephone: 1-800-PR-GREEN